FreeBSD v10 Jails - Step by Step

A ZFS Based Jail Configuration Workbook

By: Benjamin T. Hacker Jr.

Berkeley Forest Press

ISBN: 978-0-9971946-0-9

TABLE OF CONTENTS

Introduction 1

Why I Wrote this Guide 2

    Acknowledgements: 3

My Host Configuration 4

Preparing to configure the Multi-Jail Infrastructure 5

    FreeBSD v10.x 5

    Host is Z file system 5

    BuildWorld on Host is complete 5

Creating/Configuring the Multi-Jail Infrastructure 6

Creating a Single New Jail 11

Deleting a Single Jail 13

Controlling the Jails 15

    Creating a ZFS Snapshot 15

    Restoring a ZFS Snapshot 16

    Archiving a ZFS Snapshot 16

Updating a Multi-Jail Infrastructure and its Jails 18

    Assumptions 18

    Updating the Multi-Jail Infrastructure 18

FreeBSD Jail Host with Multiple Local Networks 23

Appendix 26

    [A1] Updating the FreeBSD Jail HOST system. 26

    [A2] Check for Failed Unmount When Stopping the Jails. 28

    [A3] Jail HOST Security related questions. 28

About the Author 29

How to Build A ZFS Based FreeBSD Multi-Jail Infrastructure

INTRODUCTION

This workbook will walk you through building a FreeBSD Multi-Jail Infrastructure taking advantage of facilities provided by the ZFS file system.

Jails are a type of Operating-system-level virtualization. If you need multiple independent Unix-like servers but have cost or resource hurdles to overcome, FreeBSD Jails are an excellent solution. They are lightweight when it comes to resource usage and cost. Jails are also a secure way to isolate services. If you want to understand more about the capabilities of Jails, please see the article: "FreeBSD jail" on Wikipedia. Also see chapter 14 of the FreeBSD Handbook.

ZFS is simply an awesome filesystem/volume manager. Jails supported and tightly integrated with ZFS are simply an unbeatable combination. If you need to learn more about ZFS, please see the article: "ZFS" on Wikipedia, and my favorite: http://wiki.illumos.org/download/attachments/1146951/zfs_last.pdf

WHY I WROTE THIS GUIDE

This workbook is written to specifically outline how to build and run multiple Jails on ZFS filesystem. There are many automated methods to take advantage of Jails but none of them satisfied my need to:

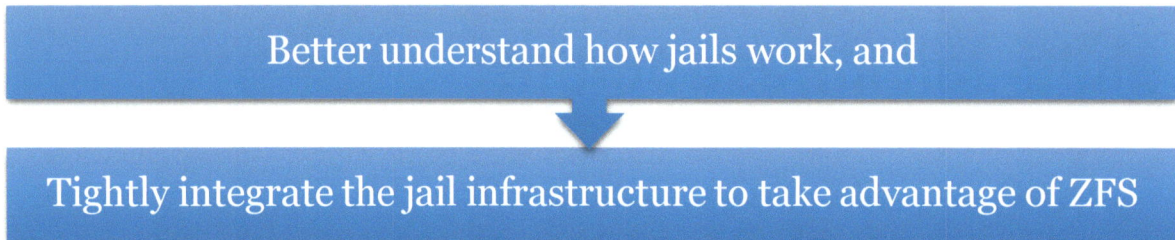

> ### Better understand how jails work, and

> ### Tightly integrate the jail infrastructure to take advantage of ZFS

I was asked in daemonforums why I don't just use EZJail, QJail or Warden to install and configure my jails. I did try all three on a FreeBSD server but they all failed for me for various reasons and my lack of understanding the basics of Jails did not help.

- ✓ Before I use any automated method, I want to install and configure manually so I learn and understand. (I want to learn Jails)

- ✓ During my last crack at ezjail and qjail... it seemed they did not take purposeful advantage of the Z File System. The instructions presented here closely integrate the Z File System.

- ✓ I also attempted the steps outlined in the Handbook chapter 14.5 (2014) but it failed due to some documentation errors or missing steps. Also, the handbook instructions do not "plan" for a Z File System. The instructions presented here closely follow those in Handbook chapter 14.5.

- ✓ Fighting through the learning process to create the instructions in this workbook solved my problems and provided a relatively "easy to maintain" Jail infrastructure.

Acknowledgements:

I would like to thank the folks that helped me verifying these instructions, proofing or publishing the document:

Sean Kidd	Malachi Rafael
Youness El Andaloussi	Bruce L. Hacker
Daniel Austin	Kyra E. Hicks

This workbook is based upon a thread I started in Sept. 2014 on DaemonForums.org. Through early 2015 I continued to post these instructions as I built this ZFS based multi-jail configuration: http://daemonforums.org/showthread.php?t=8660. I would like to thank the viewers of this forum for the more than 9000 views of this discussion thread.

"The fear of the LORD is the beginning of wisdom:
a good understanding have all they that do his commandments:
his praise endureth for ever."

Psalms 111:10
Holy Bible
King James Version

MY HOST CONFIGURATION

My physical host configuration consists of 6 drives. 2 drives are a ZFS mirrored virtual device (VDev) named: "rpool". OS is installed here. After installation of the OS, I create a second 4 drive VDev formatted using RAIDz1 named: "jpool".

In my setup, "rpool" stands for Root pool. "jpool" stands for Jail pool. There is quite a bit of space on jpool so I use it for more than just jails. For example: /jpool/distfiles dataset is mounted to /usr/ports/distfiles so "rpool" space is not wasted for any port distfiles.

I have built a similar virtual configuration on an ESXi platform creating and attaching 5 virtual hard drive's in a similar format. I have about 5 jails running under this virtual FreeBSD host.

These instructions have been tested on both virtual and physical hosts.

*Please Note! This document assumes a basic functional knowledge of running a *nix operating system in general and FreeBSD in particular.*

PREPARING TO CONFIGURE THE MULTI-JAIL INFRASTRUCTURE

These instructions assume that your server is configured with the following three conditions being true:

FreeBSD v10.x

These instructions were originally created as I installed on a FreeBSD v10.0 system. At the time of this writing the system is v10.3

Host is Z file system

These instructions substitute creating ZFS for mkdir datasets wherever possible. The advantages come into play much later in the life of the Jail when you need to make snapshots, backups and occasionally totally delete a jail.

BuildWorld on Host is complete

I continued upgrading my Host following the normal methods provided in the Handbook Ch: 23.5 and 23.6. If you are new at this see the last section called: [A1] Updating the FreeBSD system where I have listed the steps I followed.

NOTE: "cpdup" is not necessary

The Handbook introduced me to using cpdup in chapter 14.5. Some folks have asked me why I use it. I simply had not tested another way. I have now performed this installation/configuration substituting "tar" so I currently provide validated instructions that do not use cpdup.

CREATING/CONFIGURING THE MULTI-JAIL INFRASTRUCTURE

Thanks in part to: http://srobb.net/nullfsjail.html and the FBSD Handbook (Ch14)

✓	STEP 1

Create a directory structure for the read-only file system "mroot" which will contain the FreeBSD binaries for the jails.

NOTE: replace "jpool" with the name of the VDev you are using to install the jail infrastructure:

```
% su – root
# zfs create jpool/jails
# zfs create jpool/jails/j
# zfs create jpool/jails/j/mroot

# setenv D /jpool/jails/j
```

✓	STEP 2

Then, change directory to the FreeBSD source tree and install the read-only file system to the jail template:

NOTE: The following two "make" commands will take a few minutes to complete. Please wait.

```
# mkdir -p $D/mroot
# cd /usr/src
# make installworld DESTDIR=$D/mroot
# make distribution DESTDIR=$D/mroot
```

STEP 3 ✓

Prepare a FreeBSD Ports Collection for the jails as well as a FreeBSD source tree, which is required for mergemaster:

NOTE: The following "tar" command is copying source. It can take a while. Please wait.

```
# mkdir $D/mroot/usr/ports
# portsnap -p $D/mroot/usr/ports fetch extract

# cd /usr/src
# tar cf - . | ( cd $D/mroot/usr/src && tar xBpf - )
```

STEP 4 ✓

Create a skeleton for the read-write portion of the system:

NOTE: replace "jpool" with the name of the VDev you are using to install the jail infrastructure:

```
# zfs create jpool/jails/js
# zfs create jpool/jails/j/skel

# cd $D/mroot
# mkdir  $D/skel/home  $D/skel/usr-X11R6  $D/skel/distfiles
# mv etc        $D/skel
# mv usr/local $D/skel/usr-local
# mv tmp        $D/skel
# mv var        $D/skel
# mv root       $D/skel

# cp -p /etc/resolv.conf  $D/skel/etc
```

✓	STEP 5

Prepare /etc/rc.conf in each new Jail for basics

NOTE: In the following command you can replace "vi" with "ee" a simple screen oriented text editor.

```
# vi $D/skel/etc/rc.conf

  hostname="CHANGEME"
  sshd_enable="YES"
  sendmail_enable="NO"
  dumpdev="NO"
```

✓	STEP 6

Use mergemaster to install missing configuration files. Answer mergemaster by selecting defaults.

```
# mergemaster -t $D/skel/var/tmp/temproot -D $D/skel -i
```

NOTE: The mergemaster utility is a Bourne shell script which is designed to aid you in updating the various configuration and other files associated with FreeBSD. [`# man mergemaster`]

✓	STEP 7

Then, remove the extra directories that mergemaster creates:

```
# cd $D/skel
# rm -R bin boot lib libexec mnt proc rescue sbin sys usr dev
```

✓	STEP 8

Now, symlink the read-write file system to the read-only file system. Ensure that the symlinks are created in the correct /s/ locations as the creation of directories in the wrong locations will cause the installation to fail.

```
# cd $D/mroot
# mkdir s
# ln -s /s/etc         etc
# ln -s /s/home        home
# ln -s /s/root        root
# ln -s /s/usr-local   usr/local
# ln -s /s/usr-X11R6   usr/X11R6
# ln -s /s/distfiles   usr/ports/distfiles
# ln -s /s/tmp         tmp
# ln -s /s/var         var
```

✓	STEP 9

Create/edit a generic .../skel/etc/make.conf containing these lines:

NOTE: In the following command you can replace "vi" with "ee" a simple screen oriented text editor.

```
# vi $D/skel/etc/make.conf

    # This makes it possible to compile FreeBSD ports inside each jail.
    # Remember that the ports directory is part of the read-only system.
    # The custom path for WRKDIRPREFIX allows builds to be done in the
    # read-write portion of every jail

    WRKDIRPREFIX?=  /s/portbuild
```

✓	STEP 10

Enable Jails on Host by adding the following line to your /etc/rc.conf file.

NOTE: It doesn't matter where you add this line in the rc.conf file. You can add it at the end

```
# vi /etc/rc.conf

    jail_enable="YES"
```

✓	STEP 11

As a last step, Create a jail.conf config file on the Host machine.

NOTE: In the following command you can replace "vi" with "ee" a simple screen oriented text editor.

```
# vi /etc/jail.conf

    # file: /etc/jail.conf
    # Defaults
      exec.start += "/bin/sh /etc/rc";
      exec.stop = "/bin/sh /etc/rc.shutdown";
      exec.clean;
      mount.devfs;

      mount.fstab = "/etc/fstab.$name";
      exec.consolelog = "/var/log/jail_"$name"_console.log";
      host.hostname = "Jail$name";
      allow.set_hostname = 0;
    # allow.nomount;

    # Dynamic wildcard parameter:
    # Base the path off the jail name.
      path = "/jpool/jails/j/$name";

    # example {
    ##   exec.fib=0;            #: Used to select routing table
    #    interface = "lo0";
    #    ip4.addr = 127.0.0.2;
    ##   devfs_ruleset = 5;    #: Enable Jail access to NIC's
    ##    allow.sysvipc = 1;
    #    }
```

✓	STEP 12

Your Infrastructure configuration is complete! [recommend host reboot]

```
# exit
```

CREATING A SINGLE NEW JAIL

Adding a single new jail to the Multi-Jail Infrastructure. (we will assume a jail named "www") There were 9 steps to create the Multi-Jail infrastructure. Once you have the infrastructure set up there are only 4 steps to add a new jail. You can add many. You will need a static IP address for each new Jail.

✓	STEP 1

Create /etc/fstab for the new Jail:

```
% su - root
# vi /etc/fstab.www

  # Device                 Mountpoint      FStype  Options   Dump   Pass#
    /jpool/jails/j/mroot  /jpool/jails/j/www     nullfs  ro      0       0
    /jpool/jails/js/www   /jpool/jails/j/www/s  nullfs  rw      0       0
```

✓	STEP 2

Modify /etc/rc.conf to allow alias IP(s) for the Jail: (this is an example interface and static IP below)

```
# vi /etc/rc.conf

  ifconfig_em0_alias0="inet 192.168.1.51/32"
```

✓	STEP 3

Modify /etc/jail.conf with info on the new jail: (this is an example interface and static IP below)

```
# vi /etc/jail.conf      #(Add the following lines at bottom)


  www {
      #exec.fib=0;            #: Used to select routing table
      interface = "em0";
      ip4.addr += 192.168.1.51/24;
      #allow.sysvipc = 1;
      #allow.raw_sockets = 1;  # Debugging purposes
      }
      }
```

✓	STEP 4

Create the required mount points for the read-only file system of the new jail: And Install the read-write template into each jail using "tar" to copy your "skeleton" directory:

```
# mkdir /jpool/jails/j/www
# zfs create jpool/jails/js/www

# cd /jpool/jails/j/skel
# tar cf - . | ( cd /jpool/jails/js/www && tar xBpf - )
```

✓	STEP 5

Start the new jail

```
# service jail start www
```

✓	STEP 6

Log into Jail and set the Jail root user password. Also add a user account for remote access.

```
# jls
# jexec JID# tcsh
    # passwd
    # adduser
```

DELETING A SINGLE JAIL

Removing a single jail from the Multi-Jail Infrastructure. (We will assume a jail named "www")

✓	STEP 1

Stop the jail.

NOTE: Make sure all jail mounts are unmounted. (See section [A2] at the end of this document)

```
% su - root
# service jail stop www
```

✓	STEP 2

If you are concerned you may need to restore this Jail you can create a snapshot of the r/w portion of the jail, then send the snapshot to an archive file.

```
# zfs snapshot jpool/jails/js/www@Deleted`date "+%Y%m%d-%H%M" `
# zfs send jpool/jails/js/www@Deleted20150918-1728  |  gzip > /tmp/www-jail20150918.gz
```

✓	STEP 3

Delete /etc/fstab for the new Jail:

```
% su - root
# rm /etc/fstab.www        # or you can rename or move the file...
```

✓	STEP 4

Modify /etc/rc.conf to remove the alias IP(s) for the Jail:

```
# vi /etc/rc.conf      #(Remove the line(s) associated with Jail "www"

      ifconfig_em0_alias0="inet xxx.xx.xx.xx/32"
```

✓	STEP 5

Modify /etc/jail.conf by removing info on the jail being removed:

```
# vi /etc/jail.conf      #(Remove the line(s) associated with the Jail
```

✓	STEP 6

Remove the mount points for the read-only file system of the jail and destroy the read-write template. Removing the Jail is very easy when it is built on a ZFS filesystem.

```
# rm -rf /jpool/jails/j/www
# zfs destroy -r jpool/jails/js/www   # Fails if snapshots exist
```

CONTROLLING THE JAILS

These commands are run on the Jail Host:

```
# service jail start www          # (start a jail)
# service jail stop  www          # (stop  a jail)
# service jail [start | stop]     # (start or stop all jails)
# jls                             # (List running jails and their ID's)
# jexec [ID#] tcsh                # (Log into Jails console on host)
```

NOTE: Do NOT perform commands requiring network access when using jexec. The Host network configuration is enforced when using this command. If your jail is connected to a different network then its host, it will likely not function on the network while using jexec.

Currently I have 5 jails running:

ca	running a Certificate Authority
dns	
mail	
www	running Drupal
testjail	running FileLocker2

I have been working in www mostly and once I got nginx and drupal (including DB) working I needed to take a snapshot so if I goofed it up I could get back to this starting point.

Creating a ZFS Snapshot

✓ I used the following command to **create a snapshot** of the r/w portion of the jail:

o `su root -c "zfs snapshot jpool/jails/js/www@v7Drupal`date "+%Y%m%d-%H%M" ` "`

✓ You can get a **list** of all your zfs **snapshots** using:

o `zfs list -t snapshot`

I took this particular snapshot while the jail was running. Not sure if it matters if the jail is running or not but probably best if you shut it down first if you can. Only takes a second and 0 space initially.

Restoring a ZFS Snapshot

After loading a Theme and trying to run a Drupal helper called: Drush, I ended up with a "www" jail that was broken. It took some work to get my Drupal updated to v7 so rather than go thru all that again I just restored the snapshot.

- ✓ Before restoring we need to **stop the Jail**.
  - o `# service jail stop www`

NOTE: Make sure all jail mounts are unmounted. (See section [A2] at the end of this document)

- ✓ Now I can **restore** via the **snapshot** to the last good point that I had available:

```
% zfs list -t snapshot      # list all available snapshots

% su - root -c "zfs rollback jpool/jails/js/www@v7Drupal20140920-1841 "
% zfs list -t snapshot      # once restored, snapshot should be removed
% su - root -c "service jail start www "
% jls
```

When I started the jail it came up just like I had just updated to Drupal v7. Site was up and working like nothing happened, database and all!

I also snapshotted my "jpool/jails/j" which gets me my master and skeleton read only infrastructure.

Archiving a ZFS Snapshot

ZFS also has "send/receive" commands that allow you to save a snapshot to an archive file or restore a snapshot from an archive file. This facility should be good for not only archiving Jail snapshots (backups) but transferring them from one system to another.

First we "send" the stream of the snapshot through gzip to compress it and save the output from gzip to the archive file:

```
%  zfs  send jpool/jails/js/www@v739Drupal20150918-1728  |  gzip > /root/www-jail20150918.gz
```

Once you use the ZFS Send command to archive the snapshot you can safely delete the snapshot:

```
% zfs  destroy  jpool/jails/js/www@v739Drupal20150918-1728
```

To restore the snapshot you send the archive file to the ZFS Receive command.

NOTE: On the ZFS Receive command line you indicate "where" the snapshot should be restored during the future ZFS Rollback.

```
% gunzip -c /root/www-jail20150918.gz  |  zfs receive jpool/jails/js/www
```

Once the snapshot has been recreated from the archive, it can be restored to the system as shown in the previous section.

```
% zfs  rollback  jpool/jails/js/www@v739Drupal20150918-1728
```

UPDATING A MULTI-JAIL INFRASTRUCTURE AND ITS JAILS

Assumptions

In order for these steps to succeed, we are assuming these three conditions exist:

- ✓ FreeBSD v10.x – These instructions were originally created as I updated on a FreeBSD v10.x system. At the time of this writing the system is v10.3

- ✓ Host is Z Filesystem

- ✓ Updating buildworld on Host is complete (because the Jails are using same kernel as host) (See Handbook 24.5; 24.6) (See: Appendix A1)

Updating the Multi-Jail Infrastructure

✓	STEP 1

First, create a directory structure for the new/updated read-only file system which will contain the updated FreeBSD binaries for the jails:

Log into Jail Host

```
% su - root

# setenv D /jpool/jails/j

# zfs create jpool/jails/j/mroot2
# mkdir -p $D/mroot2
```

✓	STEP 2

Change directory to the FreeBSD source tree and install the read-only file system to this new jail template:

```
# cd /usr/src
# make installworld DESTDIR=$D/mroot2
# make distribution DESTDIR=$D/mroot2
```

✓	**STEP 3**

Next, prepare a FreeBSD source tree, which is required for mergemaster:

```
# cd /usr/src
# tar cf - . | ( cd $D/mroot2/usr/src && tar xBpf - )
```

✓	**STEP 4**

Create a skeleton for the read-write portion of the system:
{Of course use the correct date: skel.YYYYMMDD on the backup of old "skel"}

```
# zfs rename jpool/jails/j/skel jpool/jails/j/skel.20141120
# zfs create jpool/jails/j/skel

# cd $D/mroot2
# mkdir $D/skel/home $D/skel/usr-X11R6 $D/skel/distfiles
# mv etc        $D/skel
# mv usr/local $D/skel/usr-local
# mv tmp        $D/skel
# mv var        $D/skel
# mv root       $D/skel
```

✓	**STEP 5**

Prepare /etc/rc.conf in each new Jail for basics

```
# cp -p $D/skel.20141120/etc/rc.conf      $D/skel/etc
# cp -p $D/skel.20141120/etc/make.conf    $D/skel/etc
# cp -p $D/skel.20141120/etc/resolv.conf  $D/skel/etc
```

✓	**STEP 6**

Use mergemaster to install missing configuration files. Then, remove the extra
directories that mergemaster creates: (Just hit enter to select default in
mergemaster)

```
# mergemaster -t $D/skel/var/tmp/temproot -D $D/skel -i
# cd  $D/skel
# rm -R  bin boot  lib  libexec mnt  proc rescue sbin sys usr dev
```

✓	STEP 7

Now, symlink the read-write file system to the read-only file system. Ensure that the symlinks are created in the correct /s/ locations as the creation of directories in the wrong locations will cause the installation to fail.

```
# cd $D/mroot2
# mkdir  s
# ln -s  /s/etc          etc
# ln -s  /s/home         home
# ln -s  /s/root         root
# ln -s  /s/usr-local    usr/local
# ln -s  /s/usr-X11R6    usr/X11R6
# ln -s  /s/tmp          tmp
# ln -s  /s/var          var
```

✓	STEP 8

Now stop all running jails.

```
# service jail stop
```

NOTE: Make sure all jail mounts are unmounted. (See section [A2] at the end of this document)

✓	STEP 9

Move FreeBSD Ports Collection for the jails. Update Ports.

```
# mv $D/mroot/usr/ports $D/mroot2/usr
# portsnap -p $D/mroot2/usr/ports fetch update
```

✓	STEP 10

Backup old mroot. Install new mroot. {Of course use your own date: mroot.YYYYMMDD below}

```
# cd $D
# zfs rename jpool/jails/j/mroot  jpool/jails/j/mroot.20141120
# zfs rename jpool/jails/j/mroot2 jpool/jails/j/mroot
# exit
```

Reboot the Host

```
% su - root -c "shutdown -r now"
```

✓	STEP 11

Adding temproot to **each** (of your) existing jails

Log into Jail Host and create /var/tmp/temproot in each jail for "a later" mergemaster run.

NOTE: If the first question informs you that an old ".../temproot exists", then "Use 'd' to delete the old ".../temproot and continue".

NOTE: Just hold <Enter> key to: "leave everything for later".

```
# su - root

# mergemaster -t /jpool/jails/js/ca/var/tmp/temproot    -D /tmp/ignore
# mergemaster -t /jpool/jails/js/www/var/tmp/temproot    D /tmp/ignore
# mergemaster -t /jpool/jails/js/dns/var/tmp/temproot   -D /tmp/ignore
# mergemaster -t /jpool/jails/js/mail/var/tmp/temproot -D /tmp/ignore
# mergemaster -t /jpool/jails/js/testjail/var/tmp/temproot  -D /tmp/ignore
```

✓	STEP 12

Completing the upgrade in each Jail

Use "jls" command on jail host to check if each of the jails started and get their JID. Log into each jail from the host system.

```
# jexec [JID] tcsh
```

Run mergemaster as root within each jail to update the configuration files.

NOTE: Answer all with "i" (unless you want to change a particular configuration file.)

```
# mergemaster  -r
# exit
```

SSH into each jail and update the installed ports using either:

```
* pkg upgrade          {binary}
   -or-
* portupgrade -aR      {source}
```

NOTE: When using portupgrade, if many ports are installed and you would like to complete all the config pages prior to upgrading, use the following command first:
```
"portupgrade -a -force-config -noexecute -recursive"
```

FREEBSD JAIL HOST WITH MULTIPLE LOCAL NETWORKS

Thanks to: http://savagedlight.me/2014/03/07/freebsd-jail-host-with-multiple-local-networks

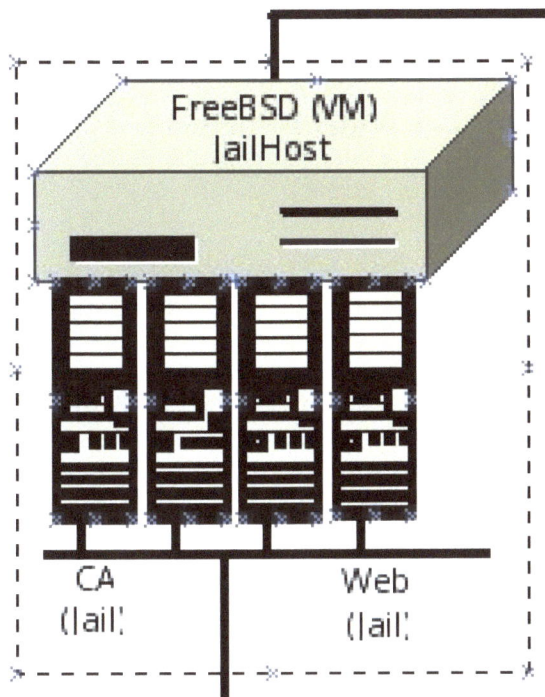

In FreeBSD you can create multiple routing tables and multiple default routes attaching them to specific network interfaces. These are also known as "Forward Information Base" or FIB, and are manipulated with the setfib utility. See: man setfib.

I was able to configure my jail host so that the Host is on my "Admin network" (top) and the Jails are on the "General network" (bottom).

Three files need to be configured:

- /boot/loader.conf

- /etc/rc.local

- /etc/jail.conf

I have two physical NIC's on my JailHost:

- em0 is my Admin network which the host communicates on.
- em1 is my General network which the Jails communicate on.

In my /boot/loader.conf I set the number of "routing tables". Max is 16, (I am supporting 2).

```
user@JailHost:~ % cat /boot/loader.conf
zfs_load="YES"
net.fibs=2
net.add_addr_allfibs=0
```

The "net.add_addr_allfibs=" configuration option in /boot/loader.conf is used to disable[0] or enable[1] adding default routes and interface routing entries to all routing tables. This should be disabled to prevent cross-talk. Default routes will automatically be added to routing table 0 which the Host uses. You will modify /etc/rc.local to establish default routes for any additional routing tables.

In /etc/rc.local you make entries to identify the default router IP for each "additional" routing table. Routing table 0 will automatically use the system defaults so it is not set in /etc/rc.local .

```
user@JailHost:~ % cat /etc/rc.local
#!/bin/sh
# file: /etc/rc.local
##
# Routing Tables
##
# 0: admin
# 1: general
#
##
# Set up the "general"[1] routing table
##
# Interface route(s)
setfib 1 route add -net 192.168.25.0/24 -iface em1
# Default route
setfib 1 route add default 192.168.25.1
```

Later in my /etc/rc.conf I will only have to reference the proper NIC em1:

```
...
ifconfig_em1_alias0="inet 192.168.25.100/32"  #www
ifconfig_em1_alias1="inet 192.168.25.120/32"  #mail
ifconfig_em1_alias2="inet 192.168.25.5/32"    #dns
...
```

Wherever you have a jail section in the Jail.conf file, you must now identify which routing table and interface the jail will use by configuring "exec.fib=" and "interface=":

```
dns {
    exec.fib=0;  # Set to the ADMIN routing table
    interface = "em0";
    ip4.addr  = 192.168.11.5/24;
    #allow.sysvipc = 1;
    }

www {
    exec.fib=1;  # Set to the GENERAL routing table
    interface = "em1";
    ip4.addr  = 192.168.25.100/24;
    #allow.sysvipc = 1;
    }
```

APPENDIX

[A1] Updating the FreeBSD Jail HOST system.

Upgrading the servers or keeping them patched is fairly simple. Patching once a month or so is good. (If this is a newly installed system you will need to install portupgrade and subversion-static using "pkg install")

Here are the steps I followed on my hosts.

NOTE: I only perform section 1a and 3.

1.   To update your list of available ported applications and all your installed ports use method "1.a" or "1.b".

   a)   **RECOMMENDED**: To update the Ports installed on the local system (Binary method)

   ```
   # pkg upgrade
   ```

   b)   **SKIP**: To update the Ports installed on the local system (Source method)

   NOTE: [We skip section 1.b because we want a "lean" host machine. If you update using portupgrade, too many other ports will be installed in order to compile the basic "portupgrade" and "subversion-static" ports.]

   More info: /usr/local/share/doc/freebsd/handbook/ports-using.html

   ```
   # portsnap fetch update
   [# portupgrade -a -force-config -noexecute -recursive ]
   # portupgrade -aR
   ```

2. **SKIP**:   To update the FreeBSD OS to current patch level (Binary method)

    NOTE: I skip section 2 because we need updated source code available for the jails.

More info:

- /usr/local/share/doc/freebsd/handbook/updating-upgrading-freebsdupdate.html

- FreeBSD security patches may be downloaded and installed using the following

```
# freebsd-update fetch
# freebsd-update install
```

3. **RECOMMENDED**: To update the FreeBSD OS to current patch level (Source method)

   a)   Download Sources and build the FreeBSD world:

```
[# svn cleanup /usr/src ]
# svn checkout svn://svn0.us-east.FreeBSD.org/base/stable/10  /usr/src
[response:] Checked out revision xxxxxx.
```

   b)   Clear out any old data in /usr/obj then build the updated OS from sources:

```
# cd /usr/src
# chflags -R noschg /usr/obj/*
# rm -rf /usr/obj

# make buildworld
```

    NOTE: Buildworld may take a couple of hours to complete.

   c)   Create a custom FreeBSD Kernel. [You can skip this if you want to use the Generic Kernel]:

```
# cd /usr/src
# cp -p sys/amd64/conf/GENERIC sys/amd64/conf/YOUR_KERNEL_HERE
# ee sys/amd64/conf/YOUR_KERNEL_HERE
```

d)   Continue with building and installing the FreeBSD Kernel

- If you skipped the: "Create a custom Kernel" above then on the lines below, delete the end of each command beginning with "KERNCONF="

```
# cd /usr/src
# make -DALWAYS_CHECK_MAKE buildkernel    KERNCONF=YOUR_KERNEL_HERE
# make -DALWAYS_CHECK_MAKE installkernel  KERNCONF=YOUR_KERNEL_HERE

<stop any running jails>
<reboot in single user mode>

See Handbook (23.6.1) step 5
# /sbin/zfs set readonly=off rpool
# /sbin/zfs mount -a

# /usr/sbin/mergemaster -p
# cd /usr/src
# make installworld

# /usr/sbin/mergemaster -i
# make delete-old
# /sbin/shutdown -r now
```

4.   These are the steps I followed on my FreeBSD v10.0 - v10.3 Jail hosts. Your mileage may vary.

[A2] Check for Failed Unmount When Stopping the Jails.

I have had some issues with my read-only mount not un-mounting automatically when the command to stop a jail is issued. Whenever you stop the jail(s) you should check to see if they properly unmounted.

```
# mount | grep "/jpool/jails/j/mroot on"
# mount | grep "/jpool/jails/j/mroot on" | grep [jailname]
```

If any are still mounted, force them to unmount:

```
# umount -f /jpool/jails/j/[jailname]
```

[A3] Jail HOST Security related questions.

For security related configuration questions please see: "14.4 Jails: Fine Tuning and Administration" in the FreeBSD Handbook.

ABOUT THE AUTHOR

Ben Hacker Jr. has worked in the IT industry for the past 35 years and has worked with FreeBSD over 15 years. He is very much a FreeBSD advocate. He also enjoys bicycle riding and singing bass in the Crossroads Baptist Church choir in Northern Virginia.

Linkedin.com/in/bhackerjr

This book was originally created on a PC running PCBSD OS and using Libre Office Writer 5.x.   *[Version 1.0]*

www.ingramcontent.com/pod-product-compliance
Lightning Source LLC
Chambersburg PA
CBHW052044190326
41520CB00002BA/185